The Len

Words for Lent & Easter

by Benedict XVI

*All booklets are published thanks to the
generous support of the members of the
Catholic Truth Society*

CATHOLIC TRUTH SOCIETY
PUBLISHERS TO THE HOLY SEE

Contents

Ash Wednesday: On the road!

Dear brothers and sisters, today, with the Ash Wednesday Liturgy, the Lenten journey of 40 days begins that will lead us to the Easter Triduum, the memorial of the passion, death and Resurrection of the Lord, heart of the mystery of our salvation. It is a favourable time when the Church invites Christians to have a keener awareness of the redeeming work of Christ and to live their Baptism in greater depth.

History of salvation

Indeed, in this liturgical season, the People of God from the earliest times have drawn abundant nourishment from the Word of God to strengthen their faith, reviewing the entire history of creation and redemption.

With its 40-day duration, Lent has an indisputably evocative power. Indeed, it intends to recall some of the events that marked the life and history of ancient Israel, presenting its paradigmatic value anew also to us.

We think, for example, of the 40 days of the great flood that led to God's Covenant with Noah, and hence, with humanity, and of the 40 days that Moses spent on Mount Sinai, after which he was given the Tablets of the Law.

The Lenten period is meant to serve as an invitation to relive with Jesus the 40 days he spent in the desert, praying and fasting, in preparation for his public mission.

Today, we too, together with all the world's Christians, are spiritually setting out towards Calvary on a journey of reflection and prayer, meditating on the central mysteries of the faith. We will thus prepare ourselves to experience, after the mystery of the Cross, the joy of Easter.

The ashes

Today, an austere and symbolic gesture is being made in all parish communities: *the imposition of ashes*, and this rite is accompanied by two formulas, full of meaning, that are a pressing appeal to recognize that we are sinners and to return to God.

The first formula says: "*Remember that you are dust, and unto dust you will return*" (cf. *Gn* 3:19). These words of the Book of Genesis call to mind the human condition placed under the sign of transience and limitation, and are meant to spur us once again to place our every hope in God alone.

The second formula refers to the words that Jesus spoke at the beginning of his itinerant ministry: "*Repent, and believe in the Gospel*" (*Mk* 1:15). This is an invitation to base our personal and community renewal on a firm and trusting attachment to the Gospel.

The Christian's life is a life of faith, founded on the Word of God and nourished by it. In the trials of life and in every temptation, the secret of victory lies in listening to the Word of truth and rejecting with determination falsehood and evil.

Listening to the Word of truth

This is the true and central programme of the Lenten Season: to listen to the word of truth, to live, speak and do what is true, to refuse falsehood that poisons humanity and is the vehicle of all evils.

It is therefore urgently necessary in these 40 days to listen anew to the Gospel, the Word of the Lord, the word of truth, so that in every Christian, in every one of us, the understanding of the truth given to him, given to us, may be strengthened, so that we may live it and witness to it.

Lent encourages us to let the Word of God penetrate our life and thus to know the fundamental truth: who we are, where we come from, where we must go, what road to take in life. And thus, the Season of Lent offers us an ascetic and liturgical route which, while helping us to open our eyes to our weakness, opens our hearts to the merciful love of Christ.

The Lenten journey, by bringing us close to God, enables us to look upon our brethren and their needs with new eyes. Those who begin to recognize God, to look at the face of Christ, also see their brother with other eyes, discover their brother, what is good for him, what is bad for him, his needs.

Love

Lent, therefore, as a time of listening to the truth, is a favourable moment to convert to love, because the deep truth, the truth of God, is at the same time love.

By converting to the truth of God, we must necessarily be converted to love; a love that knows how to make its own the Lord's attitude of compassion and mercy, as I wanted to recall in the Message for Lent, whose theme consists of the Gospel words: "Jesus, at the sight of the crowds, was moved with pity" (Mt 9:36).

Aware of her mission in the world, the Church never ceases to proclaim the merciful love of Christ, who continues to turn his compassionate gaze upon the people and peoples of every time. "In the face of the terrible challenge of poverty afflicting so much of the world's population", I wrote in the above-mentioned Message for Lent, "indifference and self-centred isolation stand in stark contrast to the 'gaze' of Christ. Fasting and almsgiving, which, together with prayer, the Church proposes in a special way during the Lenten Season, are suitable means for us to become conformed to this 'gaze'" (*L'Osservatore Romano* English edition, 8th February 2006, p.7), to the gaze of Christ, and to see ourselves, humanity, others, with his gaze.

Prayer

In this spirit, let us enter the austere and prayerful atmosphere of Lent, which is truly an atmosphere of love for our brethren.

May these be days of reflection and of intense prayer, in which we let ourselves be guided by the Word of God, which the liturgy offers to us in abundance. May Lent also be a time of fasting, penance and watchfulness of ourselves, and may we be convinced that the fight against sin is never-ending, because temptation is a daily reality and we all experience fragility and delusion.

Almsgiving

Lastly, through almsgiving and doing good to others, may Lent be an opportunity for sincere sharing with our brethren of the gifts that we have received, and of attention to the needs of the poorest and most abandoned people.

On this penitential journey, may we be accompanied by Mary, Mother of the Redeemer, who is a teacher of listening and of faithful adherence to God. May the Virgin Most Holy help us to arrive purified and renewed in mind and in spirit, to celebrate the great mystery of Christ's Pasch. With these sentiments, I wish you all a good and productive Lent.

New Heart, New Spirit

The penitential procession with which we began today's celebration has helped us enter the typical atmosphere of Lent, which is a personal and community pilgrimage of conversion and spiritual renewal.

Take up your Cross

According to the very ancient Roman tradition of Lenten *stationes*, during this season the faithful, together with the pilgrims, gather every day and make a stop - *statio* - at one of the many "memorials" of the Martyrs on which the Church of Rome is founded.

In the Basilicas where their relics are exposed, Holy Mass is celebrated, preceded by a procession during which the litanies of the Saints are sung. In this way, all those who bore witness to Christ with their blood are commemorated, and calling them to mind then becomes an incentive for each Christian to renew his or her own adherence to the Gospel.

These rites retain their value, despite the passing centuries, because they recall how important it also is in our day to accept Jesus' words without compromises: "If any man would come after me, let him deny himself and take up his cross daily and follow me" (*Lk* 9:23).

Another symbolic rite, an exclusive gesture proper to the first day of Lent, is the imposition of ashes. What is its most significant meaning?

It is certainly not merely ritualistic, but something very deep that touches our hearts. It makes us understand the timeliness of the Prophet Joel's advice echoed in the First Reading, advice that still retains its salutary value for us: external gestures must always be matched by a sincere heart and consistent behaviour.

Contrite hearts

Indeed, the inspired author wonders, what use is it to tear our garments if our hearts remain distant from the Lord, that is, from goodness and justice? Here is what truly counts: to return to God with a sincerely contrite heart to obtain his mercy (cf. *Jl* 2:12-18).

A new heart and a new spirit: we ask for this with the penitential Psalm par excellence, the *Miserere*, which we sing today with the response, "Be merciful, O Lord, for we have sinned" (*The Sunday Missal*).

The true believer, aware of being a sinner, aspires with his whole self - spirit, heart and body - to divine forgiveness, as to a new creation that can restore joy and hope to him (cf. *Ps* 51[50]:3, 5, 12, 14).

Another aspect of Lenten spirituality is what we could describe as "combative", as emerges in today's

"Collect", where the "weapons" of penance and the "battle" against evil are mentioned.

Spiritual combat

Every day, but particularly in Lent, Christians must face a struggle, like the one that Christ underwent in the desert of Judea, where for 40 days he was tempted by the devil, and then in Gethsemane, when he rejected the most severe temptation, accepting the Father's will to the very end.

It is a spiritual battle waged against sin and finally, against Satan. It is a struggle that involves the whole of the person and demands attentive and constant watchfulness.

St Augustine remarks that those who want to walk in the love of God and in his mercy cannot be content with ridding themselves of grave and mortal sins, but "should do the truth, also recognizing sins that are considered less grave..., and come to the light by doing worthy actions. Even less grave sins, if they are ignored, proliferate and produce death" (*In Io. evang.* 12, 13, 35).

Lent reminds us, therefore, that Christian life is a never-ending combat in which the "weapons" of prayer, fasting and penance are used. Fighting against evil, against every form of selfishness and hate, and dying to oneself to live in God is the ascetic journey that every

disciple of Jesus is called to make with humility and
patience, with generosity and perseverance.

Choose love

Following the divine Teacher in docility makes
Christians witnesses and apostles of peace. We might
say that this inner attitude also helps us to highlight
more clearly what response Christians should give to
the violence that is threatening peace in the world.

It should certainly not be revenge, nor hatred nor
even flight into a false spiritualism. The response of
those who follow Christ is rather to take the path chosen
by the One who, in the face of the evils of his time and
of all times, embraced the Cross with determination,
following the longer but more effective path of love.

Following in his footsteps and united to him, we
must all strive to oppose evil with good, falsehood
with truth and hatred with love.

Live for Him

In the Encyclical *Deus Caritas Est*, I wanted to present
this love as the secret of our personal and ecclesial
conversion. Referring to Paul's words to the
Corinthians, "the love of Christ urges us on" (2 *Cor*
5:14), I stressed that "the consciousness that, in Christ,
God has given himself for us, even unto death, must

inspire us to live no longer for ourselves but for him, and, with him, for others" (n. 33).

Furthermore, love, as Jesus says today in the Gospel, must be expressed in practical acts for our neighbour, and especially for the poor and the needy, always subordinating the value of "good works" to the sincerity of the relationship with our "Father who is in Heaven", who "sees in secret" and "will reward" all whose good actions are humble and disinterested (cf. *Mt* 6:1, 4, 6, 18).

An active love

The manifestation of love is one of the essential elements in the life of Christians who are encouraged by Jesus to be the light of the world, so that by seeing their "good works", people give glory to God (cf. *Mt* 5:16).

This recommendation to us is particularly appropriate at the beginning of Lent, so that we may understand better and better that "for the Church, charity is not a kind of welfare activity...but is a part of her nature, an indispensable expression of her very being" (*Deus Caritas Est*, n. 25).

True love is expressed in acts that exclude no one, after the example of the Good Samaritan who, with great openness of heart, helped a stranger in difficulty whom he had met "by chance" along the way (cf. *Lk* 10:31).

Your Eminences, venerable Brothers in the Espiscopate and in the Priesthood, dear men and women religious and lay faithful, all of whom I greet with warm cordiality, may we enter the typical atmosphere of this liturgical period with these sentiments, allowing the Word of God to enlighten and guide us.

True conversion

In Lent we will often hear re-echoing the invitation to convert and to believe in the Gospel, and we will be constantly encouraged to open our spirit to the power of divine grace. Let us cherish the abundance of teachings that the Church will be offering us in these weeks.

Enlivened by a strong commitment to prayer, determined to make a greater effort of penance, fasting and loving attention to our brethren, let us set out towards Easter accompanied by the Virgin Mary, Mother of the Church and model of every authentic disciple of Christ.

The Meaning of Lent

Dear Brothers and Sisters, the Gospel of Mark, which is the theme of the Sunday celebrations of this liturgical year, offers a catechumenal programme which guides the disciple to recognize Jesus as the Son of God.

By a fortunate coincidence, today's Gospel passage touches on the topic of fasting: as you know, next Wednesday the Lenten season begins, with the Rite of Ashes and penitential fasting. For this reason, the Gospel is particularly appropriate.

The bridegroom comes

Indeed, it recounts how while Jesus was at table in the house of Levi, the publican, the Pharisees and John the Baptist's disciples asked why Jesus' disciples were not fasting as they were. Jesus answered that wedding guests cannot fast while the bridegroom is with them and that they will fast when the bridegroom is taken away from them (cf. *Mk* 2:18, 20).

With these words, Christ reveals his identity of Messiah, Israel's bridegroom, who came for the betrothal with his people. Those who recognize and welcome him are celebrating. However, he will have to be rejected and killed precisely by his own; at that moment, during his Passion and death, the hour of mourning and fasting will come.

As I mentioned, the Gospel episode anticipates the meaning of Lent. As a whole, it constitutes a great memorial of the Lord's Passion in preparation for his Paschal Resurrection. During this season, we abstain from singing the "Alleluia" and we are asked to make appropriate penitential sacrifices.

We need a new spirit

The season of Lent should not be faced with an "old" spirit, as if it were a heavy and tedious obligation, but with the new spirit of those who have found the meaning of life in Jesus and in his Paschal Mystery and realize that henceforth everything must refer to him.

This was the attitude of the Apostle Paul who affirmed that he had left everything behind in order to know Christ and "the power of his resurrection, and [to] share his sufferings, becoming like him in his death, that if possible [he might] attain the resurrection from the dead" (*Phil* 3:10-11).

Mary teaches us

May our guide and teacher in our Lenten journey be Mary Most Holy, who followed Jesus with total faith when he set out with determination for Jerusalem, to suffer the Passion. She received like a "fresh skin" the "new wine" brought by the Son for the messianic betrothal (cf. *Mk* 2:22). And so it was that the grace she requested with a motherly instinct for the spouses at Cana, she herself had first received beneath the Cross, poured out from the pierced Heart of the Son, an incarnation of God's love for humanity (cf. *Deus Caritas Est*, nn. 13-15).

Fight against the Spirit of Evil

Dear brothers and sisters, this past Wednesday we began Lent, and today we are celebrating the first Sunday of this liturgical season that encourages Christians to set out on a path of preparation for Easter.

Today, the Gospel reminds us that Jesus, after being baptized in the River Jordan and impelled by the Holy Spirit who settled upon him and revealed him as the Christ, withdrew for 40 days into the Desert of Judea where he overcame the temptations of Satan (cf. *Mk* 1:12-13). Following their Teacher and Lord, Christians also enter the Lenten desert in spirit in order to face with him the "fight against the spirit of evil".

The desert

The image of the desert is a very eloquent metaphor of the human condition. The Book of Exodus recounts the experience of the People of Israel who, after leaving Egypt, wandered through the desert of Sinai for 40 years before they reached the Promised Land.

During that long journey, the Jews experienced the full force and persistence of the tempter, who urged them to lose trust in the Lord and to turn back; but at the same time, thanks to Moses' mediation, they learned to listen to God's voice calling them to become his holy People.

In meditating on this biblical passage, we understand that to live life to the full in freedom we must overcome the test that this freedom entails, that is, temptation. Only if he is freed from the slavery of falsehood and sin can the human person, through the obedience of faith that opens him to the truth, find the full meaning of his life and attain peace, love and joy.

A favourable time

For this very reason Lent is a favourable time for a diligent revision of life through recollection, prayer and penance. The Spiritual Exercises, which will begin this evening in accordance with tradition and continue until next Saturday here in the Apostolic Palace, will help me and my collaborators in the Roman Curia to enter with greater awareness into this characteristic Lenten atmosphere.

Dear brothers and sisters, as I ask you to accompany me with your prayers, I assure you of my remembrance to the Lord, so that Lent may be for all Christians an opportunity for conversion and a more courageous effort towards holiness. For this, let us invoke the Virgin Mary's motherly intercession.

He washes our dirty feet

"Having loved his own who were in the world, he loved them to the end" (*Jn* 13:1). God loves his creature, man; he even loves him in his fall and does not leave him to himself. He loves him to the end. He is impelled with his love to the very end, to the extreme: he came down from his divine glory.

His powerful love

He cast aside the raiment of his divine glory and put on the garb of a slave. He came down to the extreme lowliness of our fall. He kneels before us and carries out for us the service of a slave: he washes our dirty feet so that we might be admitted to God's banquet and be made worthy to take our place at his table - something that on our own we neither could nor would ever be able to do.

God is not a remote God, too distant or too great to be bothered with our trifles. Since God is great, he can also be concerned with small things. Since he is great, the soul of man, the same man, created through eternal love, is not a small thing but great, and worthy of God's love.

God's holiness is not merely an incandescent power before which we are obliged to withdraw, terrified. It is a power of love and therefore a purifying and healing power. God descends and becomes a slave, he washes our feet so that we may come to his table. In this, the entire mystery of Jesus Christ is expressed. In this, what redemption means becomes visible.

Need of purification

The basin in which he washes us is his love, ready to face death. Only love has that purifying power which washes the grime from us and elevates us to God's heights.

The basin that purifies us is God himself, who gives himself to us without reserve - to the very depths of his suffering and his death. He is ceaselessly this love that cleanses us; in the sacraments of purification - Baptism and the Sacrament of Penance - he is continually on his knees at our feet and carries out for us the service of a slave, the service of purification, making us capable of God.

His love is inexhaustible, it truly goes to the very end.

"You are clean, but not all of you", the Lord says (*Jn* 13:10). This sentence reveals the great gift of purification that he offers to us, because he wants to be at table together with us, to become our food. "But not all of you" - the obscure mystery of rejection exists, which becomes apparent with Judas' act, and precisely on Holy Thursday, the day on which Jesus made the gift of himself, it should give us food for thought. The Lord's love knows no bounds, but man can put a limit on it.

"You are clean, but not all of you": What is it that makes man unclean?

Who is Judas?

It is the rejection of love, not wanting to be loved, not loving. It is pride that believes it has no need of any purification, that is closed to God's saving goodness. It is pride that does not want to admit or recognize that we are in need of purification.

In Judas we see the nature of this rejection even more clearly. He evaluated Jesus in accordance with the criteria of power and success. For him, power and success alone were real; love did not count. And he was greedy: money was more important than communion with Jesus, more important than God and his love.

He thus also became a liar who played a double game and broke with the truth; one who lived in deceit and so lost his sense of the supreme truth, of God. In this way, he became hard of heart and incapable of conversion, of the trusting return of the Prodigal Son, and he disposed of the life destroyed.

"You are clean, but not all of you". Today, the Lord alerts us to the self-sufficiency that puts a limit on his unlimited love. He invites us to imitate his humility, to entrust ourselves to it, to let ourselves be "infected" by it.

He invites us - however lost we may feel - to return home, to let his purifying goodness uplift us and enable us to sit at table with him, with God himself.

Wash each other's feet

Let us add a final word to this inexhaustible Gospel passage: "For I have given you an example" (*Jn* 13:15); "You also ought to wash one another's feet" (*Jn* 13:14). Of what does "washing one another's feet" consist? What does it actually mean?

This: every good work for others - especially for the suffering and those not considered to be worth much - is a service of the washing of feet.

The Lord calls us to do this: to come down, learn humility and the courage of goodness, and also the readiness to accept rejection and yet to trust in goodness and persevere in it.

But there is another, deeper dimension. The Lord removes the dirt from us with the purifying power of his goodness. Washing one another's feet means above all tirelessly forgiving one another, beginning together ever anew, however pointless it may seem. It means purifying one another by bearing with one another and by being tolerant of others; purifying one another, giving one another the sanctifying power of the Word of God and introducing one another into the Sacrament of divine love.

The Lord purifies us, and for this reason we dare to approach his table. Let us pray to him to give to all of us the grace of being able to one day be guests for ever at the eternal nuptial banquet. Amen!

The Resurrection in us!

"You seek Jesus of Nazareth, who was crucified. He has risen, he is not here" (*Mk* 16:6). With these words, God's messenger, robed in light, spoke to the women who were looking for the body of Jesus in the tomb. But the Evangelist says the same thing to us on this holy night: Jesus is not a character from the past. He lives, and he walks before us as one who is alive, he calls us to follow him, the living one, and in this way to discover for ourselves too the path of life.

What is the Resurrection?

"He has risen, he is not here." When Jesus spoke for the first time to the disciples about the Cross and the Resurrection, as they were coming down from the Mount of the Transfiguration, they questioned what "rising from the dead" meant (*Mk* 9:10). At Easter we rejoice because Christ did not remain in the tomb, his body did not see corruption; he belongs to the world of the living, not to the world of the dead; we rejoice because he is the Alpha and also the Omega, as we proclaim in the rite of the Paschal Candle; he lives not only yesterday, but today and for eternity (cf. *Heb* 13:8).

But somehow the Resurrection is situated so far beyond our horizon, so far outside all our experience that, returning to ourselves, we find ourselves continuing the argument of the disciples: Of what exactly does this "rising" consist? What does it mean for us, for the whole world and the whole of history? A German theologian once said ironically that the miracle of a corpse returning to life - if it really happened, which he did not actually believe - would be ultimately irrelevant precisely because it would not concern us. In fact, if it were simply that somebody was once brought back to life, and no more than that, in what way should this concern us? But the point is that Christ's Resurrection is something more, something different. If we may borrow the language of the theory of evolution, it is the greatest "mutation", absolutely the most crucial leap into a totally new dimension that there has ever been in the long history of life and its development: a leap into a completely new order which does concern us, and concerns the whole of history.

Breaking the power of death

The discussion, that began with the disciples, would therefore include the following questions: What happened there? What does it mean for us, for the whole world and for me personally? Above all: what happened? Jesus is no longer in the tomb. He is in a totally new life. But how could this happen? What forces were in operation? The crucial point is that this man Jesus was not alone, he was not an "I" closed in upon itself. He was one single reality with the living God, so closely united with him as to form one person with him. He found himself, so to speak, in an embrace with him who is life itself, an embrace not just on the emotional level, but one which included and permeated his being. His own life was not just his own, it was an existential communion with God, a "being taken up" into God, and hence it could not in reality be taken away from him. Out of love, he could allow himself to be killed, but precisely by doing so he broke the definitiveness of death, because in him the definitiveness of life was present. He was one single reality with indestructible life, in such a way that it burst forth anew through death. Let us express the same thing once again from another angle. His death was an act of love. At the Last Supper he anticipated death and transformed it into self-giving. His existential communion with God was concretely an existential communion with God's love, and this love is the real power against death, it is stronger than death. The Resurrection was like an explosion of light, an explosion of love which dissolved the hitherto indissoluble compenetration of "dying and becoming". It ushered in a new dimension of being, a new dimension of life in which, in a transformed way, matter too was integrated and through which a new world emerges.

A qualitative leap

It is clear that this event is not just some miracle from the past, the occurrence of which could be ultimately a matter of indifference to us. It is a qualitative leap in the history of "evolution" and of life in general towards a new future life, towards a new world which, starting from Christ, already continuously permeates this world of ours, transforms it and draws it to itself. But how does this happen? How can this event effectively reach me and draw my life upwards towards itself? The answer, perhaps surprising at first but totally real, is: this event comes to me through faith and Baptism. For this reason Baptism is part of the Easter Vigil, as we see clearly in our celebration today, when the sacraments of Christian initiation will be conferred on a group of adults from various countries. Baptism means precisely this, that we are not dealing with an event in the past, but that a qualitative leap in world history comes to me, seizing hold of me in order to draw me on.

Christ lives in me

Baptism is something quite different from an act of ecclesial socialization, from a slightly old-fashioned and complicated rite for receiving people into the Church. It is also more than a simple washing, more than a kind of purification and beautification of the soul. It is truly death and resurrection, rebirth, transformation to a new life.

How can we understand this? I think that what happens in Baptism can be more easily explained for us if we consider the final part of the short spiritual autobiography that Saint Paul gave us in his *Letter to the Galatians*. Its concluding words contain the heart of this biography: "*It is no longer I who live, but Christ who lives in me*" (*Gal* 2:20). I live, but I am no longer I. The "I", the essential identity of man - of this man, Paul - has been changed. He still exists, and he no longer exists. He has passed through a "not" and he now finds himself continually in this "not": *I, but no longer I*.

Seized by the Resurrection

With these words, Paul is not describing some mystical experience which could perhaps have been granted him, and could be of interest to us from a historical point of view, if at all. No, this phrase is an expression of what happened at Baptism. My "I" is taken away from me and is incorporated into a new and greater subject. This means that my "I" is back again, but now transformed, broken up, opened through incorporation into the other, in whom it acquires its new breadth of existence. Paul explains the same thing to us once again from another angle when, in Chapter Three of the *Letter to the Galatians*, he speaks of the "promise", saying that it was given to an individual - to one person: to Christ. He alone carries within himself the whole "promise". But what then happens with us? Paul answers: You have become one in Christ (cf. *Gal* 3:28). Not just one thing, but one, one only, one single new subject. This liberation of our "I" from its isolation, this finding oneself in a new subject means finding oneself within the vastness of God and being drawn into a life which has now moved out of the context of "dying and becoming". The great explosion of the Resurrection has seized us in Baptism so as to draw us on. Thus we are associated with a new dimension of life into which, amid the tribulations of our day, we are already in some way introduced. To live one's own life as a continual entry into this open space: this is the meaning of being baptized, of being Christian. This is the joy of the Easter Vigil. The Resurrection is not a thing of the past, the Resurrection has reached us and seized us. We grasp hold of it, we grasp hold of the risen Lord, and we know that he holds us firmly even when our hands grow weak. We grasp hold of his hand, and thus we also hold on to one another's hands, and we become one single subject, not just one thing. *I, but no longer I*: this is the formula of Christian life rooted in Baptism, the formula of the Resurrection within time. *I, but no longer I*: if we live in this way, we transform the world. It is a formula contrary to all ideologies of violence, it is a programme opposed to corruption and to the desire for power and possession.

Living in God

"I live and you will live also", says Jesus in Saint John's Gospel (14:19) to his disciples, that is, to us. We will live through our existential communion with him, through being taken up into him who is life itself. Eternal life, blessed immortality, we have not by ourselves or in ourselves, but through a relation - through existential communion with him who is Truth and Love and is therefore eternal: God himself. Simple indestructibility of the soul by itself could not give meaning to eternal life, it could not make it a true life. Life comes to us from being loved by him who is Life; it comes to us from living-with and loving-with him. *I, but no longer I*: this is the way of the Cross, the way that "crosses over" a life

simply closed in on the I, thereby opening up the road towards true and lasting joy.

Thus we can sing full of joy, together with the Church, in the words of the *Exsultet*: "Sing, choirs of angels...rejoice, O earth!" The Resurrection is a cosmic event, which includes heaven and earth and links them together. In the words of the *Exsultet* once again, we can proclaim: "Christ...who came back from the dead and shed his peaceful light on all mankind, your Son who lives reigns for ever and ever". Amen!

Kindle in us the fire of your love

Dear brothers and sisters, on the day of Pentecost, the Holy Spirit descended with power upon the Apostles; thus began the mission of the Church in the world.

Jesus himself prepared the Eleven for this mission, appearing to them on many occasions after his Resurrection (cf. *Ac* 1:3).

Prior to the Ascension into Heaven, he ordered them "not to depart from Jerusalem, but to wait for the promise of the Father" (cf. *Ac* 1:4-5); that is, he asked them to *stay together* to prepare themselves to receive the gift of the Holy Spirit. And they gathered in prayer with Mary in the Upper Room, awaiting the promised event (cf. *Ac* 1:14).

Prayerful Novena

To stay together was the condition laid down by Jesus in order to receive the gift of the Holy Spirit; the premise of their harmony was prolonged prayer. In this way we are offered a formidable lesson for every Christian community.

Some think at times that missionary effectiveness depends primarily on careful programming and its subsequent intelligent application through a concrete commitment.

The Lord certainly does ask for our collaboration, but before any other response his initiative is necessary: his Spirit is the true protagonist of the Church. The roots of our being and of our action are in the wise and provident silence of God.

50 Days

The images used by St Luke to indicate the outpouring of the Holy Spirit - wind and fire - recall Sinai, where God revealed himself to the people of Israel and offered his covenant (cf. *Ex* 19:3ff.). The feast of Sinai, which Israel celebrated 50 days after the Passover, was the *feast of the Covenant*.

Speaking of the tongues of fire (cf. *Ac* 2:3), St Luke wants to show Pentecost as a new Sinai, as the *feast of the New Covenant*, where the Covenant with Israel is extended to all the nations of the earth.

The Church has been catholic and missionary from her birth. The universality of salvation is meaningfully manifested with the list of the numerous ethnic groups to which those who heard the Apostles' first proclamation belonged (cf. *Ac* 2:9-11).

The People of God, which had found its first configuration in Sinai, extends today to the point of surmounting every barrier of race, culture, space and time. As opposed to what occurred with the tower of Babel (cf. *Gn* 11:1-9), when people wanted to build a way to heaven with their hands and ended up by destroying their very capacity of mutual understanding, in Pentecost the Spirit, with the gift of tongues, demonstrates that his presence unites and transforms *confusion* into *communion*.

Human pride and egoism always create divisions, build walls of indifference, hate and violence. The Holy Spirit, on the other hand, makes hearts capable of understanding the languages of all, as he re-establishes the bridge of authentic communion between earth and heaven. The Holy Spirit is Love.

The Holy Sprirt

But how is it possible to enter into the mystery of the Holy Spirit? How can the secret of Love be understood?

The Gospel passage takes us today to the Upper Room where, after the Last Supper, a sense of loss has saddened the Apostles. This is due to the fact that Jesus' words arouse disturbing questions: He spoke of the world's hatred of him and of his own, he spoke of his mysterious departure; and there were still many other things to be said, but for the time being the Apostles were not able to bear the weight (cf. *Jn* 16:12).

To console them, he explains the meaning of his departure: he will go, but he will return; meanwhile, he will not abandon them, will not leave them orphans. He will send the Consoler, the Spirit of the Father, and the Spirit will enable them to understand that Christ's work is a work of love: love of the One who gave himself, love of the Father who has given him.

Fire of Love

This is the mystery of Pentecost: the Holy Spirit illuminates the human spirit and, by revealing Christ Crucified and Risen, indicates the way to become more like him, that is, to be "the image and instrument of the love which flows from Christ" (*Deus Caritas Est*, n. 33).

The Church, gathered with Mary as at her birth, today implores: "*Veni, Sancte Spiritus!* - Come, Holy Spirit, fill the hearts of your faithful and kindle in them the fire of your love!" Amen.

Sources

This booklet draws together homilies and addresses of Pope Benedict XVI made in 2006 during Lent and Easter:

1. *On the road* – General Audience, Ash Wednesday, 1st March 2006.
2. *New heart, new spirit* – Homily, Ash Wednesday, 1st March 2006.
3. *The meaning of Lent* – Angelus, St Peter's Square, Sunday 26th February 2006.
4. *Fight against the Spirit of Evil* - Angelus, Saint Peter's Square, First Sunday of Lent, 5th March 2006.
5. *He washes our dirty feet* – Homily, Mass of the Lord's Supper, Basilica of St John Lateran, Holy Thursday, 13th April 2006.
6. *The resurrection in us!* – Homily, Easter Vigil, Vatican Basilica, Holy Saturday, 15th April 2006.